Johannes

Vermeer

By Celeste Brusati

RIZZOLI ART SERIES

Series Editor: Norma Broude

Johannes

Vermeer

1632–1675

1. *Woman Seated at a Virginal*. c.1673–1675. Oil on canvas, 20¹/₄ x 17⁷/₈". National Gallery of Art, London

Few Old Master painters are as esteemed as Johannes Vermeer. Nearly everyone, it seems, admires the exquisite simplicity and subtle optical appeal of his pictures. Usually focused on a single figure—most often a woman—or a few figures enframed in the corner of a room deftly suffused in light, his paintings epitomize that fantasy of domestic order and tranquility that only the world of canvas and pigment can fully indulge. It has often been noted that Vermeer's pristine domestic spaces have a still-life quality. Their inhabitants rarely speak, make few gestures, and tend to be quietly absorbed in such activities as reading, writing, sleeping, making music, making lace, or simply looking. Even music-making appears to be a curiously soundless pleasure in this silent pictorial world.

Vermeer's reputation as one of the greatest artists of his day rests on an extant oeuvre of just thirty pictures. Most experts believe that he produced only about forty paintings during his twenty-year painting career. Compared to other well-known Dutch artists, including Rembrandt, Frans Hals, and such contemporary genre painters as Gerard ter Borch and Pieter de Hooch, each of whom painted hundreds of pictures during the course of his career, Vermeer was remarkably unprolific. Recent research has provided some explanations for how Vermeer managed to sustain a large family—he left his widow with eleven children when he died at the age of forty-three—on such meager production. Like many Dutch painters, he supplemented his income by dealing in art. He was also partly dependent on the wealth of his mother-in-law, Maria Thins, who came from a distinguished Catholic family from Gouda, and on the support of a Delft collector named Pieter van Ruijven. Van Ruijven, a man of independent means who held a small municipal post in Delft, owned twenty of Vermeer's pictures and was in all likelihood his patron.[1]

Vermeer's pictorial output was not only relatively small by Dutch standards, but also singularly focused. Nearly two-thirds of his works deal with amorous themes, mainly of men and women drinking wine or making music and of women reading, writing, or receiving love letters. In these works, as well as in his other domestic scenes, his townscapes, his face studies, and his rare forays into history and allegory, Vermeer always drew on well-established pictorial traditions, commenting retrospectively on popular themes rather than inventing new subject matter.

The elusive beauty of these pictures has often been described as enigmatic, poetically expressive, or reflective of the artist's innate sense of form and the "classical" harmony and purity of his designs. And yet, however much we may esteem Vermeer's artistry, there are many strange and even disturbing features of his art that too easily disappear behind such phrases. Looking at the splendid *The Art of Painting* (plate 8), for example, it is difficult to imagine a poetic or aesthetic impulse that might explain why the unarticulated mass around the painter's brush refuses to take shape as the artist's hand. Equally puzzling is the question of how a "classical" sense of order might produce the calculated spatial ambiguities of foreground and background that Vermeer introduced into such works as *A Young Woman Asleep* (plate 3) or *Maid and a Woman with a Letter* (plate 13). And terms like "poetic" or "expressive" are hardly meaningful when applied to features as curious as the masklike faces of his late pictures (fig. 1 and plates 12 and 14). Anomalies of this sort are reminders of the difficulty of characterizing Vermeer's artistic achievement, which is far more idiosyncratic—but no less compelling—than is suggested by simplified aesthetic appreciations.

The most astute of Vermeer's admirers have realized that both the idiosyncracy and the powerful appeal of his art are rooted in the distinctive artifice of his style, or what has been termed somewhat more accurately, his "vocabulary of representation."[2] Although Vermeer did not achieve the widespread fame of his more prolific contemporaries until the nineteenth century, it is clear from the high prices paid for his works and the critical judgments of them recorded in seventeenth- and eighteenth-century auction catalogues that Vermeer's usual artistry appealed to, and was highly valued by, a small group of knowledgeable connoisseurs throughout the eighteenth century.[3] Critics and commentators typically described Vermeer's distinctive style in terms of the optical qualities of his art, the way in which his pictures not only represent luminous effects, but also appear themselves to be produced by the image-making properties of light. These optical qualities are epitomized in the splendid *View of Delft* (plate 6), which is among the largest of Vermeer's pictures. The painting was purchased by the Dutch government in 1822 for the Mauritshuis Royal Cabinet of Paintings, on the occasion of the palace's transformation into a public museum. It was also the first of Vermeer's works to be publicly displayed and to attract serious critical attention from foreign visitors and aficionados of

Dutch art. It was purportedly the experience of seeing this picture that motivated the French politician and critic Etienne-Josephe Théophile Thoré to undertake the first serious research into Vermeer's oeuvre and archival remains.[4] What impressed Thoré and other early admirers of the *View of Delft* was its apparent lack of artifice, the natural quality of the light, and the apparent accuracy with which the view seemed to have been observed. Today, most scholars agree that not only the "photographic" quality of this work but also certain striking features of Vermeer's style owe something to his knowledge of the camera obscura.

This precursor of the modern photographic camera was a fairly simple apparatus, consisting of either a box or a darkened room equipped with a small aperture, usually fitted with a convex lens. When light came through the lens, a shimmering colored reflection of whatever was placed before it appeared opposite the lens on the interior wall of the box. Although these shadowy images appeared upside down and reversed from right to left, they produced an uncannily lifelike visual impression. Vermeer's contemporaries delighted in the almost magical fashion in which this device appeared to let nature paint itself. They were especially taken with the cinematic way it captured both the movement and the likeness of what it represented and allowed the viewer to gaze unseen and from a distance at life as it unfolded in front of the lens. Seventeenth-century viewers also saw the camera obscura as a technological amusement that offered knowledge of nature. On the one hand, the device was thought to demonstrate the optical process by which light formed natural images in the seeing eye. On the other hand, these images were seen as having the natural appearance that Dutch artists sought to achieve in their pictures. Samuel van Hoogstraten, a Dutch painter and writer whom Vermeer may have known personally, suggested that the camera obscura's image was a paradigm of lifelike painting and advised aspiring artists to study and imitate its pictorial reflections in order to learn how to make their own paintings appear "truly natural."[5]

It seems that Vermeer, too, took the camera obscura as a model for his own pictorial practice. His paintings' characteristic absence of delineated contours marking the boundaries of forms, abrupt disjunctions of scale and tone, and juxtapositions of focused and unfocused details, as well as his use of circular dabs of paint on darker backgrounds, which imitate the circles of halation that appear on unfocused highlights seen in optical devices, have all been cited as evidence of Vermeer's acquaintance with this image-making technology. Despite general agreement concerning Vermeer's familiarity with the camera obscura, scholars have had different ideas about its relationship to his art. Initially, it was presumed that he used the camera as a mechanical aid to produce accurate images. In recent years, the celebrated realism of Dutch art has come to be understood rather differently, less as a product of accurate transcriptions and more as a function of certain naturalizing pictorial conventions that give Dutch pictures the appearance of having been observed and faithfully recorded. This reassessment of Dutch realism has helped call attention to the ways in which the camera obscura might have provided the optical model for Vermeer's representational vocabulary itself.[6]

While it has long been thought that Vermeer used the device in making such pictures as the *View of Delft*, many scholars now realize that he did so with an eye to emulating the peculiarities of its optically produced image rather than to obtaining an accurate record of the site. In part, the *View of Delft* owes its impression of topographical accuracy to Vermeer's use of a pictorial format conventionally employed in topographical views to present the profile of a city as seen from across a river. The use of this formula itself gives the picture a factual appearance, despite Vermeer's alteration of many features of the townscape. Vermeer's adjustments are especially interesting in light of the overall effect of compression they produce. By altering rooflines and reorienting selected buildings, he gave the Delft skyline a more unified, friezelike appearance. He also collapsed spatial intervals between structures, effectively assuring that his painting would more closely resemble the look of the image formed optically in the camera obscura.[7]

Vermeer's emulation of the camera's representational means was not simply a question of style. His sustained interest in the artifice of images believed to provide empirical access to nature also raises larger questions about the kind of knowledge of the world such representations offer. Unlike Van Hoogstraten, who celebrated the descriptive and naturalizing properties of the camera obscura's pictures, Vermeer considered their possibilities with circumspection. By focusing the camera on the description of domestic life, rather than the picturing of nature, he repeatedly posed the pictorial question of what its optical artifice might reveal or conceal when directed at human subjects. Pictures that exemplify his optical method, like his haunting *Head of a Girl Wearing a Turban and Pearl Earring* (plate 7), are among the most poignant of Vermeer's meditations on the elusiveness and intangibility of what we can know by way of images made by the action of light reflected on a surface, whether in the eye or on the canvas. In this respect, Vermeer's representational concerns diverged from those of contemporary genre painters, including Van Hoogstraten, Ter Borch, Dou, and Metsu, with whom he is often compared. In place of their imitative virtuosity, Vermeer's paintings reveal a gradual breaking down of those conventions of naturalism that his contemporaries had refined to such an extraordinary degree in their works. In the course of his pictorial investigations, he moved from the clotted and crusty facture of such pictures as the *Woman Reading a Letter at an Open Window* (plate 4), with its tiny bright dots of reflected light glittering on the sleeve and hair of the letter reader, to the smoothly laid on patches of color that characterize his handling of paint in pictures from the 1670s (plates 11–15). Over the years, Vermeer gradually reduced his descriptive means to something like a "bare optical statement," adopting a seemingly impartial method of tonally mapping (rather than modeling) the myriad surfaces and textures in his mature works. The oddly disjointed patterns of tone visible in many of Vermeer's late pictures ultimately destroy the descriptive transparency of the naturalist convention his colleagues worked so hard to maintain.

Vermeer explicitly made the analogy between the optical basis of his own representational craft and that of the camera obscura in his diminutive *The Lace-Maker* (plate 11), a tiny work of less than ten by eight inches. Both its small format and its close-up approach invite the viewer to lavish on the picture the kind of attention that the lace-maker gives to her painstaking task. Upon close scrutiny the picture

2. Nicolaes Maes. *The Lace-Maker*. 1655.
Oil on panel, 22³/₄ x 17¹/₄". National Gallery
of Canada, Ottawa

reveals not only the craft of the lace-maker, but also that of
the painter, who has set up a complex interplay between his
own artistry and hers, most conspicuously in details such as
the juxtaposition of the razor-sharp lines of the threads she
works with her bobbins and the more loosely articulated
threads of paint spilling out of the sewing cushion in the
left foreground. The optical craftedness of the image is
accentuated by the circular dots of paint that represent the
unfocused highlights on the threads and on the lace collar,
the flat patches of pigment that constitute her braid, and the
juxtaposition of the crisply focused plane of the blank wall
in the background with the numerous out-of-focus features
of the figure and her accoutrements. Vermeer's insistence
on the artifice of his method is all the more evident when
his *The Lace-Maker* is compared to a fairly typical rendition
of this subject by Nicolaes Maes (fig. 2). Vermeer not only
removed much of the descriptive incident so fully articulated in the Maes painting, he also concentrated the greatest
optical ambiguity in the figure itself, insisting that we see
disjointed flat patches of color where we would most hope
and expect to find a seamlessly modeled hand, arm, or face.

As the above example suggests, questions of pictorial
means and interrelated meanings are never totally separa-
ble, least of all in Vermeer's work, where representational
issues are played out thematically in his choice and treat-
ment of subjects. The vast majority of Vermeer's paintings
present familiar genre scenes transformed into pictorial
meditations on what might be called the erotics of representation. In these pictures he invites us to consider the attention paid by a male artist to a female subject. Sometimes he
examines this relationship vicariously, as in his depictions
of men attending visually to their female companions (plate
5). Most often, however, it is the staging of each scene that
draws our attention to conditions under which the artist sus-
tains his gaze—and the viewers'—upon female subjects.
The single-mindedness with which he was able to explore
this problem may owe something to the fact that so many
of his works appear to have been done with the support of
a single patron. It is not clear just how these pictures reflect
his patron Van Ruijven's interests, but without substantial
financial backing it seems unlikely that Vermeer would
have had the opportunity to investigate these issues in such
a sustained and consistent way.

An unsuspecting visitor to the Mauritshuis might well be
surprised to find alongside the *View of Delft* and the much-
beloved *Head of a Girl Wearing a Turban and Pearl Earring*
(plate 7) the painting *Diana and Her Companions* (plate 1)
also by Vermeer's hand. His earliest works were, in fact,
large-scale biblical and mythological pictures quite different in size and style from the small cabinet pieces we usually associate with his name.[8] Yet even in these early history
pictures, we can see him exploring thematic concerns that
run throughout his work. In the *Diana*, for example, Vermeer
looks at the dangers of transgressive viewing via the tragic
myth of Actaeon, the young hunter who paid with his life
for accidentally spying on the chaste goddess at her bath.
As punishment for straying into the sacred grotto, which
was closed to the male gaze by the goddess's proscription,
Actaeon was transformed into a stag and then consumed
by his own dogs, who took him for prey. Vermeer has
approached the subject with some delicacy, showing the
goddess of the hunt enjoying a foot bath in the company of
her nymphs. He has presented both Diana and her entourage
clothed rather than bathing in the nude, as they usually
appear in mythological paintings. The few conspicuous bits
of flesh he does include, such as the oddly illuminated
breasts of the goddess, suggest more the painter's discom-
fort than sensual pleasure in painting them. Perhaps most
strikingly, he has put himself and the viewer into Actaeon's
place: we are the illicit beholders. Lest we fail to note that
substitution, Vermeer has included subtle reminders of
Actaeon's tragic fate in the form of a dog, the animal which
ultimately consumed the hunter, gazing at a thistle, a traditional symbol of transience.

Vermeer's repeated and somewhat reticent depictions of
women in interiors suggest a similar awareness of the intru-
sive nature of the painter's gaze as he paints these domestic
versions of Diana's chaste realm. It is interesting to think
about *The Procuress* (plate 2) of 1656 in the context of his
ongoing concern with the erotics of representation. This
life-size picture, which is his earliest dated extant work, is
rightly described as a bridge between the large-scale history
paintings that precede it and the smaller cabinet pieces
that follow it. Its format and subject matter derive from the
work of a group of Utrecht painters, including Hendrick Ter
Bruggen, Dirck van Baburen, and Gerrit Honthorst, who
were known for their half-length pictures of the sensual
pleasures and dangers of the bordello and tavern. Their
works, like the genre pictures by Caravaggio to which they
are related, were much sought after by collectors at the
time. Vermeer's early interest in their work may be related
to the likelihood of his training in Utrecht.[9] We also know
that an inventory of the common property of Vermeer's in-
laws included a painting of a procuress by Van Baburen,
which was later transferred to Vermeer's mother-in-law's
house in Delft.[10] Vermeer, who lived for a time with his family in that house, included this painting as an accessory on
the wall in at least two of his paintings, the *Concert* (former-
ly in the Gardner Museum) and the *Woman Seated at a
Virginal* (fig. 1). In his version of the subject, Vermeer
departed from his prototypes in various ways, most notably
in the figure of the procuress, normally a wrinkled old hag,
but here shown as a figure of indeterminate sex in black
with a smooth, masklike face that bears a remarkable
resemblance to that of the male patron about to make his

transaction. Sexual innuendoes concerning the character of this exchange are discreetly represented in the accessories—like the lute neck and glasses held by the figures and the suggestively folded apron of the woman whose sexual favors are being purchased. Vermeer conspicuously omitted the exposed fleshy bosom that usually identifies the prostitute figures in these scenes of sex for sale. The man who drops the coin into her hand while grasping her breast is perhaps the most striking figure of all, for he is the only male figure in a Vermeer painting who actually touches a woman in a frankly sexual way. Even as he does so, the illusory nature of his grasp becomes evident as the soft form of her breast begins to dissolve between his fingers. It is difficult to imagine this man with his fingers dripping in paint as anyone but Vermeer's surrogate. If he is, what is the nature of their transaction? Is he paying for her sexual services or for posing as his model—and therefore for the erotic pleasure he takes in sustaining his gaze upon her while he paints?

In subsequent works Vermeer played out his relation to his model in terms of his gaze upon, rather than his grasp of, his subject. In the *A Young Woman Asleep* (plate 3), for example, Vermeer uses the woman sleeping as a device for gazing at her. She is, one might say, painted in the guise of "stilled life," like the objects piled up around her. Iconographic readings of this picture, which focus on the proverbial and moral associations of sleeping figures with the vice of sloth, tend to avoid the issue of Vermeer's deployment of sleep as a pictorial strategy for observing his human subject. Vermeer's interest in the masking and unmasking aspects of this theme are evident in his juxtaposition of the mask-like face of the sleeping woman with the portion of a painting visible behind it showing a discarded mask at the foot of a cupid. We might believe that Vermeer was less concerned with making a moral judgment upon the woman's wine-induced sleep and more with alerting us to the unmasking of her amorous dreams and his own eroticized gaze.

In the slightly later *Woman Reading a Letter at an Open Window* (plate 4), Vermeer frames his attention to his subject within the conventions of the popular amorous theme of the love letter, showing the female object of his gaze absorbed in reading a message of love, rather than dreaming of it. He suggestively pairs the elusive reflection of the woman's head in the window with the letter below it, as if to draw a comparison between the pictorial image wrought by his desire and that image of the beloved figured in the lover's missive. In its optical presence this mirror image of the woman resembles the mirror image above the head of the woman in A *Lady at the Virginals with a Gentleman* (plate 5). Here Vermeer has made the popular theme of the music lesson or music-making couple an occasion for looking at the rapt visual attention a man lavishes on a woman, who seems only to return that gaze indirectly. Within the ebony-framed rectangle at the farthest remove from the viewer we can see not only a suggestion of the woman's reciprocal gaze, but also what appear to be the legs of the painter's easel. Thus, bracketed off in this tonally rendered image is the optical artifice that would become his new way of painting. Vermeer gave a human face to this artifice in his compelling *Head of a Girl Wearing a Turban and Pearl Earring* (plate 7). Here it is the vagaries of tone rather than the certainties of delineation that produce an image that

epitomizes the fragility of the eye's and the painter's optical hold on the visible world that "truly natural painting" claims to capture.

All but a few of Vermeer's interiors feature mirrors, pictures, or maps on the walls. The inclusion of such details is not surprising given the popularity of these forms of pictorial wall decoration in Holland at the time. These depicted images also have—along with other interior furnishings—richly inventive signifying functions. As early as the 1860s, Théophile Thoré recognized that the accessories in Vermeer paintings, particularly the pictures on the walls, were of some significance. Much of the writing on Dutch genre pictures in the last two decades has sought to interpret these accessories with reference to their similarity to the images found in the Dutch emblem books popular in Holland during Vermeer's time. These illustrated books were essentially collections of images furnished with captions and commentaries. The emblematic texts have been thought to provide the interpretive key to explaining the meanings of pictorial motifs, which appear both in paintings and in emblems. For example, the frequent appearance of marine paintings in pictures of women reading letters has been linked to love emblems in which an image of a boat at sea is accompanied by a verse comparing the beloved to a ship and the course of love to the sea. Thus, in pictures like Gabriel Metsu's *A Woman Reading a Letter* (fig. 3) the presence of a seascape

3. Gabriel Metsu. *A Woman Reading a Letter*. c.1666–1667. Oil on canvas, 20½ x 16". Courtesy the National Gallery of Ireland, Beit Collection

on the wall alerts the beholder to the amorous nature of the letter, as well as to the steadiness or storminess of the relationship between the sender and the recipient of the missive. In his painting treatise, Van Hoogstraten praised the ingenious use of emblems and accessories to "covertly explain something" and described this practice as a form of pictorial writing through which painters could wittily make the hidden passions and emotions of their figures visible and legible.[11] What is remarkable about Dutch genre painting is the extent to which artists entrusted the task of describing human feelings and interactions to these cleverly disposed accessories rather than to the human figure itself.

Perhaps more than any of his compatriots Vermeer seems to have understood what was at stake in choosing to signify complex human emotions in this way. In his so-called *Love*

Letter (plate 13), he literally put a frame around the popular theme of a woman receiving a love letter and its emblematic apparatus to comment upon it pictorially. Vermeer staged the scene of a woman conversing with her maid in a brightly lit room behind the rectangular borders of an open doorway, from which a curtain has been raised. Although Vermeer's picture is replete with emblematic accessories, they complicate rather than elucidate the unfolding narrative. Emblems of domesticity, such as the broom, slippers, and needlework, are arrayed with the lute, the music, and the paintings on the wall—all of which have amorous connotations. Indeed some of these accessories can refer to both spheres of activity. Vermeer has left ambiguous whether the woman's unopened letter is being sent or received. By the same token, his use of the marine painting and the pastoral landscape on the wall behind suggests how neither image elucidates the contents of the letter or the substance of the conversation between the woman and her maid.

Vermeer availed himself of the representational devices often used to introduce emblematic meanings into pictures. He thereby framed commentaries on the art of painting itself. Far from providing straightforward keys to the interpretation of his images, however, the paintings on the walls of Vermeer's pictures pose questions and generate meanings in a variety of ways. Sometimes he used them to draw formal and thematic parallels between the human interactions described in his pictures and the depicted images behind them, as in the case of the *A Young Woman Asleep* (plate 3) and the St. James's Palace *A Lady at the Virginals with a Gentleman* (plate 5), in which the attendance of the gentleman on the lady at the virginals is paralleled to the dependent relationship of the captive figure of the elderly Cimon suckling at his daughter's breast in the painting on the wall.[12] On other occasions Vermeer depicted a given picture in several different contexts, such as a large cupid holding a love letter, which X rays show that he painted out of the Dresden *Woman Reading a Letter at an Open Window* (plate 4) but which appears in the *Woman Standing at the Virginals* (plate 14) and the *Music Lesson* in the Frick Collection. He also displayed the Van Baburen *Procuress* twice, once in the Boston *Concert* and again in the *Woman Seated at a Virginal*. The *Finding of Moses*, which is writ large on the wall of his *Woman Writing a Letter with Her Maid* (plate 12), appears again in a more diminutive format in *The Astronomer* (plate 9). Interpreters looking for emblematic meanings in Vermeer's work have given far more attention to the content of these pictures than to the meaningfully nuanced ways in which Vermeer has represented them. Sometimes he cropped out a specific fragment, other times he juxtaposed them strategically with maps, mirrors, depicted images, and other representational elements in his paintings. Many commentators have been all too ready to presume that Vermeer's depicted paintings were meant as moral commentaries on the scenes before them—that *The Finding of Moses* in *The Astronomer* alludes to biblical proscriptions against astronomy, for example, or that the *Last Judgment* in the *Woman Holding a Balance* (plate 10) was intended to be a moral judgment upon the vanity of her absorption in the worldly matters.

In recent years interpreters have been more inclined to consider questions of meaning in these works in broader terms.[13] In studies of Vermeer's very accurate depictions of cartographic materials in his pictures, the scientific activity of *The Astronomer* has been linked by way of the picture on the wall with Moses' knowledge of the wisdom of Egypt, which included astronomy and geography. Likewise, the darkened mirror, the empty scales, and the painting of the weighing of souls in the *Woman Holding a Balance* have been connected to her pregnancy and read as references to the undetermined fate of her unborn child's soul. Some of the most provocative readings of his pictures have sought to examine how Vermeer used emblematic conventions to bracket and juxtapose different forms of pictorial artistry and call attention to the kinds of meanings each produces. Several critics have suggested how Vermeer used such depicted paintings to point to pictorial subjects and concerns that are excluded from his optically rendered scenes of domestic life.[14] Seen in this context, Vermeer's *Woman Holding a Balance* offers a powerful meditation on the relationship between the empirical visual judgment exercised by the woman checking the justness of her balance scale and the moral judgement enacted in the large painting of the final weighing of souls in the *Last Judgment* depicted on the wall behind her. In juxtaposing the figure of the woman with the depicted history painting, Vermeer visually frames a comparison between two kinds of painting and two ways of understanding the world, one rooted in the judgments of the eye and the other grounded in judgments and considerations of a moral order.

Nowhere did Vermeer use this strategy more explicitly to reflect on his own art than in his ambitious *The Art of Painting*, in which he paired a marvelously ornate historical wall map with a model posing as Clio, the Muse of History. In doing so he was making a pointed comparison between two radically different ways of pictorially representing history, one descriptive and geographical and the other figural and allegorical. Many features of this work, especially such obviously allegorical trappings as the book, trumpet, and laurel crown that identify the figure as the Muse of History, have led commentators to treat this picture as a straightforward allegory. Yet Vermeer did not really paint an allegory. Instead he produced a commentary on the making of allegorical representations, by lifting the curtain on the pictorial process through which allegories are crafted in the studio. The studio he describes is not just any studio, but one that closely resembles the domestic spaces in which Vermeer typically set his pictures. The painter, who wears so-called Burgundian costume of the sixteenth century, is as much on stage as his dressed-up model. Though not a literal self-portrait of Vermeer, the painter nonetheless represents Vermeer's artistry by demonstrating his manner of tonally mapping out the colored shapes of the leaves in the model's crown. Just as the unformed hand of the artist makes us see the limits of Vermeer's optical method, his staging of an allegory-in-the-making calls our attention to the pictorial artifice by which allegorical meanings themselves are produced.

To return to the question of the appeal of Vermeer's art, it seems that its visual interest cannot be reduced to what might be seen as beautiful or poetical in any conventional sense. Much of what is compelling about his meticulously crafted pictures, with all their optical idiosyncrasies, lies in the depth of feeling with which he meditated on the limitations of the descriptive artistry thought to be "truly natural" by his contemporaries. Perhaps better than any other Dutch genre painter, he reminds us of the complexities of life and meaning that will always elude that art's optical net.

NOTES

(For short citations, refer to Further Reading)
Special thanks to the graduate students in my seminars at the University of Michigan and Northwestern University for stimulating discussions on Vermeer, and to Jennifer Robertson for her critical reading of this essay.

1. J. Michael Montias gives a detailed and fascinating account of the archival story of Vermeer's family and professional connections in *Vermeer's Milieu. A Web of Social History.*
2. This phrase was coined by Lawrence Gowing in his book *Vermeer.* Gowing's study remains one of the most acute critical appreciations of Vermeer. This essay owes much to Gowing's insights as well as to the critical writings of Alpers, Berger, Nash, and Snow, each of whom develop aspects of Gowing's assessment of Vermeer.
3. On the appreciation of Vermeer in the seventeenth and eighteenth centuries, see Albert Blankert, *Vermeer of Delft: Complete Edition of the Paintings.* (Oxford: Phaidon, 1978), pp. 60–67.
4. Thoré conducted his research on Vermeer while in political exile, and published his findings under the name of W. Bürger. He published a short essay and catalog in W. Bürger, *Musées de la Hollande, II, Musée van der Hoop à Amsterdam et Musée de Rotterdam* (Brussels/Ostende: 1860), pp. 67–88. The bulk of his research appeared in a series of articles in the *Gazette des Beaux-Arts,* xxi (1866), pp. 297–330, 458–470, 542–575.
5. Samuel van Hoogstraten, *Inleyding tot de hooge schoole der schilderkonst, anders de zichtbaere werelt* ["Introduction to the Academy of Painting, or the Visible World"] (Rotterdam: 1678), p. 263.
6. This rethinking of Dutch realism was given particular impetus by the revisionist account of Northern art presented in Alpers's influential study *The Art of Describing.* Alpers argued that the look of Dutch pictures and their compelling fiction of having been observed and recorded was the product of descriptive artifice rather than exact transcription. Within her account she presents Vermeer as the premier artist who reflected on the implications of making pictures that present themselves as descriptions of the world seen in this way.
7. Vermeer's manipulations of the topographic features of the *View of Delft* are discussed in Arthur Wheelock and C.J. Kaldenbach, "Vermeer's *View of Delft* and his Vision of Reality," *Artibus et Historiae* 3 (1982), pp. 9–35.
8. In addition to the *Christ in the House of Martha and Mary* in Edinburgh and the Mauritshuis *Diana,* a *St. Praxedis,* painted after an Italian picture, has been recently attributed to Vermeer. See Wheelock, "*St. Praxedis*: New Light on the Early Career of Vermeer."
9. Montias discusses a number of good reasons for thinking that Vermeer spent time in Amsterdam and Utrecht during his formative years in *Vermeer and His Milieu,* pp. 98–107.
10. The inventory was drawn up as part of the legal separation Maria Thins obtained from her abusive husband, Willem Bolnes. Montias gives the details of this separation and the events leading up to it, as well as documentation concerning the Van Baburen picture in *Vermeer and His Milieu,* pp. 116–122.
11. Van Hoogstraten, p. 88.
12. This picture, which depicts the story of the Roman prisoner Cimon, who was condemned to die by starvation and was suckled by his daughter Pero, may be the painting of "one who sucks the breast," mentioned in the inventory of pictures belonging to Vermeer's mother-in-law.
13. Examples include: Edward Snow, *A Study of Vermeer*; Harry Berger, "Conspicuous Exclusion"; Nanette Salomon, "Vermeer and the Balance of Destiny"; James Welu, "Vermeer's *Astronomer.*"
14. Most notably Alpers, Berger, Gowing, and Snow.

FURTHER READING

Aillaud, G., A. Blankert, and J. M. Montias. *Vermeer.* Paris: Hazan, 1986.

Alpers, Svetlana. *The Art of Describing.* Chicago: University of Chicago Press, 1983.

Berger, Harry. "Conspicuous Exclusion in Vermeer. An Essay in Renaissance Pastoral." *Yale French Studies* 47 (1972), pp. 243–265.

_____. "Some Vanity of His Art: Conspicuous Exclusion." *Salmagundi* 44–45 (Spring–Summer 1979), pp. 89–113.

Blankert, Albert. With contributions by Rob Ruurs and Willem van de Watering. *Vermeer of Delft: Complete Edition of the Paintings.* Oxford: Phaidon, 1978.

Gowing, Lawrence. *Vermeer.* New York: Harper and Row, 1977 [first edition 1952].

Montias, John Michael. *Artists and Artisans in Delft. A Socio-Economic Study of the Seventeenth Century.* Princeton: Princeton University Press, 1986.

_____. *Vermeer and His Milieu. A Web of Social History.* Princeton: Princeton University Press, 1989.

Nash, John. *Vermeer.* London: Scala Books in association with the Rijksmuseum, Amsterdam, 1991.

Pops, Martin, ed. *Vermeer. An Anthology of Criticism. Salmagundi* 44/45 (1979).

Salomon, Nanette. "Vermeer and the Balance of Destiny." in *Essays in Northern European Art Presented to Egbert Haverkamp-Begemann.* Doornspijk: Davaco Publishers, 1983.

Slatkes, Leonard. *Vermeer and His Contemporaries.* New York, 1981.

Snow, Edward. *A Study of Vermeer.* Berkeley and Los Angeles: University of California Press, 1979.

Welu, James. "Vermeer: His Cartographic Sources." *Art Bulletin* 57 (1975), pp. 529–547

_____. "Vermeer's *Astronomer*: Observations on an Open Book." *Art Bulletin* 68 (1986), pp. 263–267.

Wheelock, Arthur K., Jr. *Perspective, Optics and Delft Artists around 1650.* New York: Garland Press, 1978.

_____. "Vermeer's *View of Delft* and His Vision of Reality." *Artibus et Historiae* 3, no. 6 (1982), pp. 9–35.

_____. "St. Praxedis: New Light on the Early Career of Vermeer." *Artibus et Historiae* 7 (1986), pp. 71–89.

_____. *Vermeer.* Second edition, New York: Harry N. Abrams, 1988.

First published in 1993 in the United States of America by Rizzoli International Publications, Inc.
300 Park Avenue South
New York, New York 10010

Library of Congress Cataloging-in-Publication Data
Brusati, Celeste
    Vermeer/by Celeste Brusati.
        p. cm.—(Rizzoli Art Series)
    Includes bibliographical references and index
    ISBN 0-8478-1649-4
    1. Vermeer, Johannes, 1632–1675—Criticism and interpretation.
I. Title. II. Series.
ND653.V5B78 1993
759.9492—dc20   92–36644
                                                                CIP

Series Editor: Norma Broude
Series designed by José Conde and Betty Lew/Rizzoli

Printed in Italy

Front cover: see colorplate 4

Index to Colorplates

1. *Diana and Her Companions.* c.1655–1656. This is one of Vermeer's few history paintings. By the 1660s history paintings only appear in Vermeer's work in the form of depicted pictures that adorn the walls in his paintings of domestic interiors.

2. *The Procuress.* 1656. So-called scenes of mercenary love were popular in Dutch genre painting. Vermeer's unusual rendition of this subject avoids the anecdotes of seduction and deception typically found in such scenes and centers on the monetary transaction that the viewer witnesses along with the other figures in the picture.

3. *A Young Woman Asleep.* c.1657–1658. In this picture Vermeer exploits the device of the *doorkijk*, or view seen through an open doorway or threshold, which Dutch genre painters often used to multiply areas of visual interest in their pictures. Autoradiographs taken of this painting show that Vermeer painted over the figure of a dog situated at the entrance to this secondary space and replaced the portrait of a man with the mirror next to the window on the back wall.

4. *Woman Reading a Letter at an Open Window.* c.1657–1658. This is the earliest of Vermeer's depictions of epistolary themes and, as in the *Woman Asleep*, shows his tendency to place multiple barriers between himself and his subject. X rays show that Vermeer altered this picture as well, by removing a large *roemer* from the foreground and a painting from the wall.

5. *A Lady at the Virginals with a Gentleman.* c.1662–1664. This picture marks a transitional moment for Vermeer within this work. The thick and crusty facture of his earlier cabinet pieces is evident in the figures and furnishings of the room, while the mirror and depicted painting on the wall show the smooth tonal method he would adopt in his mature works.

6. *View of Delft.* c.1660–1661. Although this famous picture belongs within a tradition of profile views of cities seen from the opposite bank of a river, Vermeer's optical refinement transforms that tradition. When it was auctioned in 1822, the picture was described as "the most excellent and famous painting of this master" and "absolutely unique of its kind."

7. *Head of a Girl Wearing a Turban and Pearl Earring.* c.1662–1665. The optical ambiguities that Vermeer's tonal method introduces into this picture are easily lost on the modern viewer conditioned to reading photographic images, but they must have been quite striking to Vermeer's contemporaries.

8. *The Art of Painting.* c.1665–1667. This is not only one of Vermeer's most ambitious works, but also one which had special value for his widow, Catharina Bolnes. Shortly after his death, she tried to keep the picture in the family's possession by transferring it to her mother, Maria Thins, supposedly in partial payment of Vermeer's debts to her.

9. *The Astronomer.* 1668. This picture may have been intended to be a companion piece to *The Geographer* in the Städelsches Kunstinstitut in Frankfurt. In 1713 both pictures were described as depicting "mathematical artists." Vermeer may well have identified aspects of his descriptive artistry with theirs.

10. *Woman Holding a Balance.* c.1662–1665. Until recently this picture retained its traditional title of a "Woman Weighing Gold." By showing a woman visually judging the accuracy of an empty scale, Vermeer shifts attention from vanity of gold weighing to matters of judgment and balance.

11. *The Lace-Maker.* c.1668–1670. This tiny canvas is one of the finest of Vermeer's later works, and one of his most complex pictorial statements on the painter's craft. It formed part of the collection of paintings belonging to Pieter van Ruijven, which was passed to his son-in-law Jacob Dissius and sold at auction in 1696.

12. *Woman Writing a Letter with Her Maid.* c.1670–1672. Many of the optical anomalies seen in *The Lace-Maker* appear in this work as well. This is presumably the same picture that Vermeer's widow gave (along with the *Guitar Player* in the Iveagh Bequest at Kenwood) to the baker Hendrick van Buyten to settle a debt.

13. *Maid and a Woman with a Letter (The Love Letter).* c.1669–1670. The view into a room seen from behind a threshold became a popular format in Dutch genre painting of the 1660s and 1670s. Such a picture shows a fascination with covert viewing similar to that expressed in commentaries on the camera obscura's furtive images.

14. *Woman Standing at the Virginals.* c.1673–1675. This late work offers a rare example of the woman who is the focus of Vermeer's pictorial attention looking back at the artist. She stands poised at the virginal before a picture of Cupid as if awaiting a signal from the artist/beholder to begin their duet.

15. *Allegory of the Faith.* c.1673–1674. Described in 1718 as a "sitting woman with many meanings, representing the New Testament," this is one of Vermeer's most unusual works. Like *The Art of Painting*, it points out the uneasy relationship between Vermeer's descriptive artistry and the production of allegorical meanings.

1. *Diana and Her Companions.* c.1655–1656. Oil on canvas, 38³/₄ x 41³/₈". Photograph ©Mauritshuis, The Hague

2. *The Procuress*. 1656. Oil on canvas, 56¹/₈ x 51¹/₈".
Staatliche Kunstsammlungen, Gemäldegalerie, Dresden

3. *A Young Woman Asleep.* c.1657–1658. Oil on canvas, 34½ x 30⅛".
The Metropolitan Museum of Art, New York. Bequest of Benjamin Altman, 1913

4. *Woman Reading a Letter at an Open Window*. c.1657–1658. Oil on canvas, 32³/₄ x 25³/₈".
Staatliche Kunstsammlungen, Gemäldegalerie, Dresden

5. *A Lady at the Virginals with a Gentleman*. c.1662–1664. Oil on canvas, 28⁷/₈ x 25³/₈".
Royal Collection, St. James's Palace ©H.M. Queen Elizabeth II

6. *View of Delft*. c.1660–1661. Oil on canvas, 38³/₄ x 46¹/₄".

7. *Head of a Girl Wearing a Turban and Pearl Earring.* c.1662–1665. Oil on canvas, 18¹/₄ x 15³/₄".
Photograph ©Mauritshuis, The Hague

8. The Art of Painting. c.1665–1667. Oil on canvas, 47¼ x 39⅜".
Kunsthistorisches Museum, Vienna

9. *The Astronomer*. 1668. Oil on canvas, 19⅝ x 17¾".
Musée du Louvre, Paris. Giraudon/Art Resource, New York

10. *Woman Holding a Balance*. c.1662–1665. Oil on linen, 16³/₄ x 15".
Widener Collection, ©1992 National Gallery of Art, Washington D.C.

11. *The Lace-Maker*. c.1668–1670. Oil on canvas attached to panel, 9⅝ x 8¼".
Musée du Louvre, Paris. Scala/Art Resource, New York

12. *Woman Writing a Letter with Her Maid.* c.1670–1672. Oil on canvas, 28 x 23".
National Gallery of Ireland, Dublin, Beit Collection

13. *Maid and a Woman with a Letter (The Love Letter)*. c.1669–1670. Oil on canvas, 17³/₈ x 15¹/₈".
Rijksmuseum-Stichting, Amsterdam

14. *Woman Standing at the Virginals*. c.1673–1675. Oil on canvas, 20³/₈ x 17³/₄".
Reproduced by courtesy of the Trustees, The National Gallery, London

15. *Allegory of the Faith*. c.1673–1674. Oil on canvas, 45 x 35".
The Metropolitan Museum of Art, New York. Bequest of Michael Friedsam, 1931. The Friedsam Collection